The Essence of Wisdom

BROADWAY BOOKS
NEW YORK

The *Essence* of *Wisdom*

Words from the Masters

to Illuminate the

Spiritual Path

EDITED BY

Stephen Mitchell

BROADWAY

Library of Congress Cataloging-in-Publication Data
The essence of wisdom : words from the masters to illuminate the spiritual path / edited by Stephen Mitchell. — 1st ed.
p. cm.
Includes bibliographical references.
ISBN 0-7679-0305-6
1. Spiritual life—Quotations, maxims, etc. I. Mitchell, Stephen, 1943– .
BL624.E87 1998   98-17856
291.4'32—dc21   CIP

FIRST EDITION

Designed by George Brown

98 99 00 01 02 10 9 8 7 6 5 4 3 2 1

To Michael Katz

The sayings collected here embody the essence of spiritual wisdom. Each of them, though partial, is complete. Through each part you can see the whole.

I have arranged the sayings in a kind of impromptu progression, from the earlier steps along the path to the full embodiment of wisdom. But in spiritual practice, the elementary is often the elemental, and the first step may also turn out to be, at a deeper level, the last step. So although page Y in this book has a higher number than page X, it may not present a more profound or a more refined insight. The progression isn't necessarily linear. It is meant to be taken lightly.

Nevertheless, there is a vast difference in experience between some of the earlier sayings and some of the later ones. Take, for example, the saying I have put at the beginning and the one at the end. "In the struggle between yourself and the world," Kafka says, "second the world." Yün-men, when asked what is the essence of wisdom, says, "When spring comes, the grass grows by itself." Kafka's is a wonderful saying, with an exquisite sense of timing: it perches the ego out on a limb and then has it, like a cartoon character, saw itself off in mid-air. The humor is deadly serious, though, and the advice goes deep, as anyone knows who has had even a glimpse of the intelligence of the universe. But even to take sides against the ego is to assume the struggle, and thus to be forever involved in it. How far this is from the effortless serenity of Yün-men, where the mind has become an element as natural as sunlight or rain. And how do we get from point alpha to point omega? "This thing we tell of can never be found by seeking," says the Sufi Master Bistami, "yet only seekers find it."

The Essence of Wisdom is not meant to be read as you would read most books. Each saying stands alone on an otherwise empty page because, in order to resonate deeply, it needs at least that much emptiness around it. (If the economics of publishing were different, each saying would have its own book.) Each is a meditation in itself, enough for a day's reading; you might try reading one at the beginning of your day, then carrying it with you in your mind, lightly, as the day progresses, and reading it again just before you go to sleep. Even better: rather than reading them, I hope you can find a way to let these sayings read you. Wherever you don't understand them, and wherever you *do* understand, let them keep ripening in the empty spaces inside you. The more open you are, the more they will bear fruit.

The Essence of Wisdom

In the struggle between yourself and the world, second the world.

Franz Kafka

We are close to waking up when we dream that we are dreaming.

Novalis

Our "original mind" includes everything within itself. It is always rich and sufficient within itself. You should not lose your self-sufficient state of mind. This does not mean a closed mind, but actually an empty mind and a ready mind. If your mind is empty, it is always ready for anything; it is open to everything. In the beginner's mind there are many possibilities; in the expert's mind there are few.

Shunryu Suzuki, Rōshi

M ost people have turned their solutions toward what is easy and toward the easiest side of the easy; but it is clear that we must trust in what is difficult; everything alive trusts in it, everything in Nature grows and defends itself any way it can and is spontaneously itself, tries to be itself at all costs and against all opposition. We know little, but that we must trust in what is difficult is a certainty that will never abandon us.

Rainer Maria Rilke

The truth can be spoken only by someone who already lives inside it; not by someone who still lives in untruth and only sometimes reaches out from untruth toward it.

Ludwig Wittgenstein

If you bring forth what is inside you, what you bring forth will save you. If you don't bring forth what is inside you, what you don't bring forth will destroy you.

The Gospel of Thomas

The fact that our task is exactly as large as our life makes it appear infinite.

Franz Kafka

E very man's condition is a solution in hieroglyph to those inquiries he would put. He acts it as life before he apprehends it as truth.

Ralph Waldo Emerson

Reality is simply the loss of the ego. Destroy the ego by seeking its identity. It will automatically vanish and reality will shine forth by itself. This is the direct method.

There is no greater mystery than this, that we keep seeking reality though in fact we *are* reality. We think that there is something hiding our reality and that it must be destroyed before reality is gained. How ridiculous! A day will dawn when you will laugh at all your past efforts. That which will be on the day you laugh is also here and now.

Ramana Maharshi

We have no reason to harbor any mistrust against our world, for it is not against *us*. If it has terrors, they are *our* terrors; if it has abysses, these abysses belong to us; if there are dangers, we must try to love them. And only if we arrange our lives in accordance with the principle which tells us that we must always trust in the difficult, what now appears to us as the most alien will become our most intimate and trusted experience. How could we forget those ancient myths that stand at the beginning of all races, the myths about dragons that at the last moment are transformed into princesses? Perhaps all the dragons in our lives are princesses who are only waiting to see us act, just once, with beauty and courage. Perhaps everything that frightens us is, in its deepest essence, something helpless that wants our love.

Rainer Maria Rilke

It is proper to doubt. Do not be led by holy scriptures, or by mere logic or inference, or by appearances, or by the authority of religious teachers. But when you realize that something is unwholesome and bad for you, give it up. And when you realize that something is wholesome and good for you, do it.

The Buddha

If the place I want to arrive at could only be reached by a ladder, I would give up trying to arrive at it. For the place I really have to reach is where I must already be.

What is reachable by a ladder doesn't interest me.

Ludwig Wittgenstein

The struggle between good and evil
is the primal disease of the mind.

Seng-ts'an

I would like to beg you to have patience with everything un-resolved in your heart and to try to love *the questions them-selves* as if they were locked rooms or books written in a very foreign language. Don't search for the answers, which could not be given to you now, because you would not be able to live them. And the point is, to live everything. *Live* the ques-tions now. Perhaps then, someday far in the future, you will gradually, without even noticing it, live your way into the answer.

Rainer Maria Rilke

In what concerns divine things, belief is not appropriate. Only certainty will do. Anything less than certainty is unworthy of God.

Simone Weil

The way up and the way down are one and the same.

Heraclitus

No one doubts that he exists, though you may doubt the existence of God. If you find out the truth about yourself and discover your own source, this is all that is required.

Ramana Maharshi

For this pattern which I give you today is not hidden from you, and is not far away. It is not in heaven, for you to say, "Who will go up to heaven and bring it down for us, so that we can hear it and do it?" Nor is it beyond the sea, for you to say, "Who will cross the sea and bring it back for us, so that we can hear it and do it?" But the teaching is very near you, it is in your mouth and in your heart, so that you can do it.

The Bible

The kingdom of God is within you.

Jesus of Nazareth

From within or from behind, a light shines through us upon things and makes us aware that we are nothing, but the light is all.

Ralph Waldo Emerson

A man walking along a high road sees a great river, its near bank dangerous and frightening, its far bank safe. He collects sticks and foliage, makes a raft, paddles across the river, and reaches the other shore. Now suppose that, after he reaches the other shore, he takes the raft and puts it on his head and walks with it on his head wherever he goes. Would he be using the raft in an appropriate way? No; a reasonable man will realize that the raft has been very useful to him in crossing the river and arriving safely on the other shore, but that once he has arrived, it is proper to leave the raft behind and walk on without it. This is using the raft appropriately.

In the same way, all truths should be used to cross over; they should not be held on to once you have arrived. You should let go of even the most profound insight or the most wholesome teaching; all the more so, unwholesome teachings.

The Buddha

God's grace is the beginning, the middle, and the end. When you pray for God's grace, you are like someone standing neck-deep in water and yet crying for water. It is like saying that someone neck-deep in water feels thirsty, or that a fish in water feels thirsty, or that water feels thirsty.

Ramana Maharshi

The Master is available to all people
and doesn't reject anyone.
He is ready to use all situations
and doesn't waste anything.
This is called embodying the light.

What is a good man but a bad man's teacher?
What is a bad man but a good man's job?
If you don't understand this, you will get lost,
however intelligent you are.
It is the great secret.

Lao-tzu

The whole of wisdom is contained in two Biblical statements: "I am that *I AM*" and "Be still and know that I am God."

Ramana Maharshi

We lie in the lap of immense intelligence, which makes us receivers of its truth and organs of its activity.

Ralph Waldo Emerson

When Hui-hai first came to Zen Master Ma-tsu, Ma-tsu asked him, "What have you come here for?"

Hui-hai said, "I have come seeking the Buddha's teaching."

"What a fool you are!" Ma-tsu said. "You have the greatest treasure in the world inside you, and yet you go around asking other people for help. What good is this? I have nothing to give you."

Hui-hai bowed and said, "Please, tell me what this treasure is."

Ma-tsu said, "Where is your question coming from? *This* is your treasure. It is precisely what is asking the question at this very moment. Everything is stored in this precious treasure-house of yours. It is there at your disposal, you can use it as you wish, nothing is lacking. You are the master of everything. Why then are you running away from yourself and seeking for things outside?"

Upon hearing these words, Hui-hai realized his own mind.

Once, the great Ma-tsu said to me, "Your own treasure-house already contains everything you need. Why don't you use it freely, instead of chasing after something outside yourself?" From that day on, I stopped looking elsewhere. Just make use of your own treasure-house according to your needs, and you will be happy men. There isn't a single thing that can be grasped or rejected.

When you stop thinking that things have a past or future, and that they come or go, then in the whole universe there won't be a single atom that is not your own treasure. All you have to do is look into your own mind; then the marvelous reality will manifest itself at all times.

Hui-hai

You are alone with everything you love.

Novalis

Your true nature is not lost in moments of delusion, nor is it gained at the moment of enlightenment. It was never born and can never die. It shines through the whole universe, filling emptiness, one with emptiness. It is without time or space, and has no passions, actions, ignorance, or knowledge. In it there are no things, no people, and no buddhas; it contains not the smallest hairbreadth of anything that exists objectively; it depends on nothing and is attached to nothing. It is all-pervading, radiant beauty: absolute reality, self-existent and un-created. How then can you doubt that the buddha has no mouth to speak with and nothing to teach, or that the truth is learned without learning, for who is there to learn? It is a jewel beyond all price.

Huang-po

This thing we tell of can never be found by seeking, yet only seekers find it.

Abu Yazid al-Bistami

Without beginning or ending, your original wisdom has been shining forever, like the sun. To know whether or not this is true, look inside your own mind.

Padmasambhava

The breeze from the pine woods makes my robe flutter;
the moon above the mountain shines on my guitar.
You ask me to explain the reason for success or failure.
The fisherman's song dives deep into the river.

Wang Wei

We loosely talk of Self-realization, for lack of a better term. But how can one real-ize or make real that which alone is real? All we need to do is to give up our habit of regarding as real that which is unreal. All religious practices are meant solely to help us do this. When we stop regarding the unreal as real, then reality alone will remain, and we will be that.

Ramana Maharshi

The Great Way isn't difficult
          for those who are unattached to their preferences.
Let go of longing and aversion,
          and everything will be perfectly clear.

Seng-ts'an

You ask me, "How shall I think upon God himself, and what is he?" To this I cannot answer you, except to say, "I don't know."

For with your question you have brought me into that same darkness and into that same cloud of unknowing that I want *you* to be in. For of all other creatures and their works— yes, and of the works of God himself—a man may through grace have fullness of knowing, and he can well think upon them; but upon God himself, no man can think. And therefore I wish to leave everything I can think, and choose for my love that thing which I cannot think. Because he may well be loved, but not thought. By love he may be gotten and held; but by thinking, never.

The Cloud of Unknowing

The Tao is the law of nature, which you can't depart from even for one instant. If you could depart from it, it wouldn't be the Tao. Thus the mature person looks into his own heart and respects what is unseen and unheard. Nothing is more manifest than the hidden; nothing is more obvious than the unseen. Thus the mature person pays attention to what is happening in his inmost self.

Tzu-ssu

When you realize the unborn, uncreated, unconditioned, you are liberated from everything born, created, and conditioned.

The Buddha

For one human being to love another human being: that is perhaps the most difficult task that has been entrusted to us, the ultimate task, the final test and proof, the work for which all other work is merely preparation.

Rainer Maria Rilke

When you meet the Buddha, kill the Buddha.

Lin-chi

D o your work, then step back.
The only path to serenity.

Lao-tzu

All bodhisattvas should develop a pure, lucid mind that doesn't depend upon sight, sound, touch, flavor, smell, or any thought that arises in it. A bodhisattva should develop a mind that alights nowhere.

The Diamond Sutra

Marriage is the highest mystery.

Novalis

The point of marriage is not to create a quick commonality by tearing down all boundaries; on the contrary, a good marriage is one in which each partner appoints the other to be the guardian of his solitude, and thus they show each other the greatest possible trust. A merging of two people is an impossibility, and where it seems to exist, it is a hemming-in, a mutual consent that robs one party or both parties of their fullest freedom and development. But once the realization is accepted that even between the closest people infinite distances exist, a marvelous living side by side can grow up for them, if they succeed in loving the expanse between them, which gives them the possibility of always seeing each other as a whole and before an immense sky.

Rainer Maria Rilke

A monk asked Zen Master Tung-shan, "When heat and cold come, how can we escape from them?"

Tung-shan said, "Why don't you go to the place where there is neither heat nor cold?"

The monk said, "What place is that?"

Tung-shan said, "When it is hot, you die of heat. When it is cold, you die of cold."

S tep aside from all thinking,
        and there is nowhere you can't go.

Seng-ts'an

You might ask, "How can I know if something is God's will?" My answer is, "If it were not God's will, it wouldn't exist even for an instant; so if something happens, it *must* be his will." If you truly enjoyed God's will, you would feel exactly as though you were in the kingdom of heaven, whatever happened to you or didn't happen to you.

Meister Eckhart

The scientist's religious feeling takes the form of a rapturous amazement at the harmony of natural law, which reveals an intelligence of such superiority that, in comparison with it, the highest intelligence of human beings is an utterly insignificant reflection. This feeling is the guiding principle of his life and work.

Albert Einstein

In the pursuit of knowledge,
every day something is added.
In the practice of the Tao,
every day something is dropped.
Less and less do you need to force things,
until finally you arrive at non-action.
When nothing is done,
nothing is left undone.

Lao-tzu

The mind should be kept independent of any thoughts that arise within it. If the mind depends upon anything, it has no sure haven.

The Diamond Sutra

The more you understand yourself and your emotions, the more you necessarily love God.

Baruch Spinoza

In the archer there is a resemblance to the mature person. When he misses the bullseye, he turns and seeks the reason for his failure in himself.

Confucius

Even the most enlightened beings, even the holiest saints, make mistakes. But whereas foolish people cover up their mistakes and keep on making the same ones, the wise correct their mistakes and never make the same ones twice. The ability to correct our mistakes and to change ourselves is called wisdom.

Unattributed

A single atom of the sweetness of wisdom in a man's heart is better than a thousand pavilions in Paradise.

Abu Yazid al-Bistami

In the world of things as they are,
    there is no self, no non-self.
If you want to describe its essence,
    the best you can say is "Not-two."
In this "Not-two," nothing is separate,
    and nothing in the world is excluded.

Seng-ts'an

D on't be confused by surfaces; in the depths everything becomes law.

Rainer Maria Rilke

Sincerity is the fulfillment of our own nature, and to arrive at it we need only follow our true self. Sincerity is the beginning and end of existence; without it, nothing can endure. Therefore the mature person values sincerity above all things.

Sincerity is not only the fulfillment of our own being; it is also the quality through which all beings are fulfilled. When we fulfill our own being, we become truly human; when we fulfill all beings, we arrive at true understanding. These qualities—humanity and understanding—are inherent in our nature, and by means of them we unite the inner and the outer. Thus, when we act with sincerity, everything we do is right.

Tzu-ssu

Nothing is done by chance or by accident, but all by the foreseeing wisdom of God. If it be chance or accident in the sight of man, our blindness and unforesight is the cause. Thus I understood in this revelation of love, for I well know that in the sight of our lord God there is no chance or accident; wherefore I had to grant that all things that are done are well done, for our lord God does them all.

Dame Julian of Norwich

When you realize where you come from,
you naturally become tolerant,
disinterested, amused,
kindhearted as a grandmother,
dignified as a king.
Immersed in the wonder of the Tao,
you can deal with whatever life brings you,
and when death comes, you are ready.

Lao-tzu

Every time that we say "Thy will be done," we should have in mind all possible misfortunes added together.

Simone Weil

Our bodily food is changed into us, but our spiritual food changes us into itself.

Meister Eckhart

M en are admitted into heaven not because they have curbed and governed their passions or have no passions, but because they have cultivated their understandings. The treasures of heaven are not negations of passion, but realities of intellect, from which all the passions emanate uncurbed in their eternal glory.

William Blake

Justice is not postponed. A perfect equity adjusts its balance in all parts of life. The dice of God are always loaded. The world looks like a multiplication table, or a mathematical equation, which, turn it how you will, balances itself. Take what figure you will, its exact value, nor more nor less, still returns to you. Every secret is told, every crime is punished, every virtue rewarded, every wrong redressed, in silence and certainty.

Ralph Waldo Emerson

It is our right to hate the actions of an evil man, but because his deepest self is the image of God, it is our duty to honor him with love.

Abraham Isaac Kook

I take my own intelligence as my teacher.

A-Ni-Ko

I have just three things to teach:
simplicity, patience, compassion.
These three are your greatest treasures.
Simple in actions and in thoughts,
you return to the source of being.
Patient with both friends and enemies,
you accord with the way things are.
Compassionate toward yourself,
you reconcile all beings in the world.

Lao-tzu

God wants nothing from you but the gift of a peaceful heart.

Meister Eckhart

Anyone whose reward from God is deferred until tomorrow has not truly worshiped Him today.

Abu Yazid al-Bistami

He who binds to himself a joy
Does the winged life destroy.
But he who kisses the joy as it flies
Lives in eternity's sun rise.

William Blake

If the mind is happy, not only the body but the whole world will be happy. So you must find out how to become happy yourself. Wanting to reform the world without discovering your true self is like trying to cover the whole world with leather to avoid the pain of walking on stones and thorns. It is much simpler to wear shoes.

Ramana Maharshi

The disciples said to him, "When will the repose of the dead happen, and when will the new world come?" Jesus said, "What you are waiting for has already come, but you don't recognize it."

The Gospel of Thomas

It is easy to keep things at a distance; it is hard to be naturally beyond them.

Bunan

For the mature person, the Tao begins in the relation between man and woman, and ends in the infinite vastness
of the universe.

Tzu-ssu

Every thing possible to be believed is an image of truth.

William Blake

Gaining enlightenment is like the moon reflected on the water. The moon doesn't get wet; the water isn't broken. Although its light is broad and great, the moon is reflected even in a puddle an inch wide. The whole moon and the whole sky are reflected in one dewdrop on the grass.

Enlightenment doesn't destroy the person, just as the moon doesn't break the water. The person doesn't hinder enlightenment, just as a dewdrop doesn't hinder the moon in the sky. The depth of the dewdrop is the height of the moon. The time of the reflection, long or short, proves the vastness of the dewdrop, and the vastness of the moon in the sky.

Dōgen

God continually showers the fullness of his grace on every being in the universe, but we consent to receive it to a greater or lesser extent. In purely spiritual matters, God grants all desires. Those who have less have asked for less.

Simone Weil

The farther you enter into the truth, the deeper it is.

Bankei

If the doors of perception were cleansed, every thing would appear to man as it is: infinite.

William Blake

The ancient Masters slept without dreams and woke up without worries. Their food was plain. Their breath came from deep inside them. They didn't cling to life, weren't anxious about death. They emerged without desire and reentered without resistance. They came easily; they went easily. They didn't forget where they were from; they didn't ask where they were going. They took everything as it came, gladly, and walked into death without fear. They accepted life as a gift, and they handed it back gratefully.

Chuang-tzu

To study Buddhism is to study the self. To study the self is to forget the self. To forget the self is to be enlightened by all things. To be enlightened by all things is to drop off our own body and mind, and to drop off the bodies and minds of others. No trace of enlightenment remains, and this no-trace continues endlessly.

Dōgen

The Messiah will come only when he is no longer necessary.

Franz Kafka

Jesus saw some infants nursing. He said to his disciples, "These infants are like those who enter the kingdom of heaven." They said to him, "How then can we enter?" Jesus said to them, "When you make the two one, and when you make the inside like the outside, and the outside like the inside, and the upper like the lower, and when you make male and female into a single one, then you will enter the kingdom."

The Gospel of Thomas

All the way to heaven is heaven.

Catherine of Siena

You shall love the Unthinkable with all your heart and with all your mind and with all your strength. And these words which I command you today shall be upon your heart; and you shall teach them to your children, and speak of them when you sit in your house and when you walk on the road and when you lie down and when you rise up; and you shall bind them as a sign upon your hand and they shall be like a pendant between your eyes; and you shall write them upon the doorposts of your house and upon your gates.

The Bible

Why did the ancient Masters esteem the Tao?
Because, being one with the Tao,
when you seek, you find;
and when you make a mistake, you are forgiven.
That is why everybody loves it.

Lao-tzu

Self is everywhere, shining forth from all beings,
vaster than the vast, subtler than the most subtle,
unreachable, yet nearer than breath, than heartbeat.
Eye cannot see it, ear cannot hear it nor tongue
utter it; only in deep absorption can the mind,
grown pure and silent, merge with the formless truth.
As soon as you find it, you are free; you have found yourself;
you have solved the great riddle; your heart forever is at peace.
Whole, you enter the Whole. Your personal self
returns to its radiant, intimate, deathless source.

Mundaka Upanishad

Wherever you turn is God's face.

Muhammad

To men, some things are good and some are bad. But to God, all things are good and beautiful and just.

Heraclitus

The Now in which God created the first man and the Now in which the last man will disappear and the Now in which I am speaking—all are the same in God, and there is only one Now.

Meister Eckhart

In all ten directions of the universe,
there is only one truth.
When we see clearly, the great teachings are the same.
What can ever be lost? What can be attained?
If we attain something, it was there from the beginning of
    time.
If we lose something, it is hiding somewhere near us.

Ryōkan

The supreme perfection of giving consists in the threefold purity. Here a bodhisattva gives a gift, and he does not perceive a self who gives, a receiver, or a gift; also no reward for his giving. He surrenders that gift to all beings, but he perceives neither beings nor self. He dedicates that gift to enlightenment, but he does not perceive any such thing as enlightenment. This is called the supreme perfection of giving.

The Perfection of Wisdom Sutra

When the truth doesn't fill our body and mind, we think we have had enough. When the truth fills our body and mind, we realize that something is missing. For example, when we look at the ocean from a boat, with no land in sight, it seems circular and nothing else. But the ocean is neither round nor square, and its features are infinite in variety. It is like a palace. It is like a jewel. Only to our eyes, only for a moment, does it seem circular. All things are like this. Although there are numberless aspects to all things, we see only as far as our vision can reach. And in our vision of all things, we must appreciate that although they may look round or square, the other aspects of oceans or mountains are infinite in variety, and that universes lie all around us. It is like this everywhere, right here, in the tiniest drop of water.

Dōgen

To see a World in a Grain of Sand
And a Heaven in a Wild Flower,
Hold Infinity in the palm of your hand
And Eternity in an hour.

William Blake

The entire visible universe is the Buddha; so are all sounds. Hold fast to one principle and all the others are identical. On seeing one thing, you see all things. On perceiving any individual's mind, you perceive all mind. Glimpse one truth, and all truth is present in your vision, for there is nowhere at all that is devoid of the Truth. When you see a grain of sand, you see all possible worlds, with all their vast rivers and mountains. When you see a drop of water, you see the nature of all the waters of the universe.

Huang-po

The eye through which I see God is the same eye through which God sees me; my eye and God's eye are one eye, one seeing, one knowing, one love.

Meister Eckhart

Mind has no color, is neither long nor short, doesn't appear or disappear; it is free from both purity and impurity; it was never born and can never die; it is utterly serene. This is the form of our original mind, which is also our original body.

Hui-hai

One instant is eternity;
eternity is in the now.
When you see through this one instant,
you see through the one who sees.

Wu-men

Perfection is another name for reality.

Baruch Spinoza

The goal of wisdom is laughter and play—not the kind that one sees in little children who do not yet have the faculty of reason, but the kind that is developed in those who have grown mature through both time and understanding. If someone has experienced the wisdom that can only be heard from oneself, learned from oneself, and created from oneself, he does not merely participate in laughter: he becomes laughter itself.

Philo

The place is here; the way leads everywhere.

Dōgen

A monk once asked Zen Master Yün-men, "What is the essence of the Supreme Teaching?"

Yün-men said, "When spring comes, the grass grows by itself."

A-Ni-Ko (n.d.), Nepalese metal-founder and craftsman. His statement was in response to a question from Kublai Khan (1216–1294).

Abu Yazid Tayfur ibn 'Isa ibn Surushan al-Bistami (?–c. 874), Persian mystic, founder of the ecstatic school of Sufism.

Bankei (1622–1693), Japanese Zen Master.

The Bible (final recension: 7th–3rd? century B.C.E.), the selections are from Deuteronomy.

Blake, William (1757–1827), English visionary, poet, and artist.

The Buddha ("The Awakened One"), Gautama Siddhartha (c. 563–c. 483 B.C.E.), Indian monk, teacher, and religious reformer.

Bunan (1603–1676), Japanese Zen Master; worked as a gatekeeper until his forties.

Catherine of Siena (1347–1380), Christian mystic and saint.

Chuang-tzu (369?–286? B.C.E.), Chinese Taoist Master, philosopher, and comedian.

The Cloud of Unknowing (mid- to late 14th century), written by an anonymous English monk sometime between 1349 and 1395.

Confucius (551–479), Chinese philosopher.

The Diamond Sutra (4th century), written in India; the greatest of the Mahayana Buddhist scriptures.

Dōgen Kigen (1200–1253), Japanese Zen Master, philosopher, poet, painter, founder of the Soto Zen school in Japan.

Eckhart, Meister Johannes (1260–1327), German priest and theologian, the most insightful of Christian teachers.

Einstein, Albert (1879–1955), German-Jewish physicist and Zionist.

Emerson, Ralph Waldo (1803–1882), American essayist and poet.

The Gospel of Thomas (1st–2nd century), a collection of sayings attributed to Jesus. Fragments of the original Greek text were discovered in Egypt at the turn of this century, and a Coptic translation of the complete text turned up in 1945, along with other important Gnostic manuscripts.

Heraclitus (6th–5th century B.C.E.), Greek philosopher.

Huang-po Hsi-yun (?–849), Chinese Zen Master.

Hui-hai Ta-chu (8th century), Chinese Zen Master.

Jesus of Nazareth (4? B.C.E.–30? C.E.), Jewish prophet, healer, and religious reformer.

Julian of Norwich, Dame (1343–?), English anchoress; there is evidence that she was still alive in 1416.

Kafka, Franz (1883–1924), Czech-Jewish novelist and short-story writer.

Kook, Abraham Isaac (1865–1935), Jewish mystic, first chief rabbi of British Palestine.

Lao-tzu (571?–? B.C.E.), Chinese Taoist Master, possibly legendary.

Lin-chi (c. 810–867?), Chinese Zen Master, founder of the Lin-chi (Rinzai) school.

Ma-tsu Tao-i (709–788), Chinese Zen Master.

Muhammad (570?–632), Arabian prophet and religious reformer, founder of Islam.

Novalis (1772–1801), nom de plume of Friedrich von Hardenberg, German poet, metallurgist, and aphorist.

Padmasambhava (8th century), Indian monk who, at the invitation of the king of Tibet, brought Buddhism from India to Tibet in 747.

The Perfection of Wisdom Sutra (c. 100 B.C.E.–c. 100 C.E.), Mahayana Buddhist scripture.

Philo (c. 20 B.C.E.–c. 50 C.E.), Alexandrian-Jewish philosopher and Biblical exegete.

Ramana Maharshi (1879–1950), Indian sage (*maharshi* means "great sage").

Rilke, Rainer Maria (1875–1926), German poet, widely acknowledged as the greatest poet of the twentieth century.

Ryōkan (1758–1831), Japanese Zen Master, hermit, calligrapher, and poet.

Seng-ts'an (?–606), Chinese monk, the Third Patriarch of Zen.

Spinoza, Baruch (1632–1677), Dutch-Jewish philosopher and Biblical scholar; according to Bertrand Russell, he is "the noblest and most lovable of the great philosophers."

Suzuki, Shunryu, Rōshi (1905–1971), Japanese Zen Master, one of the first authentic Buddhist teachers to live in the West.

Tung-shan Liang-chieh (807–869), Chinese Zen Master, founder of the Ts'ao-Tung (Soto) school of Zen.

Tzu-ssu (483–402 B.C.E.), philosopher, grandson of Confucius.

The Upanishads (8th?–5th? centuries B.C.E.), along with the *Bhagavad Gita*, the central texts of the Hindu religion. Traditional Indian scholars date them around 1500 B.C.E.

Wang Wei (699–759), Chinese poet, painter, and musician.

Weil, Simone (1909–1943), French-Jewish philosopher, Christian theologian, sociologist, and political activist.

Wittgenstein, Ludwig (1889–1951), Austrian-Jewish philosopher.

Wu-men Hui-k'ai (1183–1260), Chinese Zen Master, author of *The Gateless Barrier*, the most widely used koan textbook.

Yün-men Wen-yen (?–949), Chinese Zen Master.

SUGGESTIONS FOR FURTHER READING

More extensive selections from some of these teachers can be found
in *The Enlightened Heart: An Anthology of Sacred Poetry,* edited by
Stephen Mitchell, HarperCollins, 1989, and *The Enlightened Mind: An
Anthology of Sacred Prose,* edited by Stephen Mitchell, HarperCollins,
1991.

Abu Yazid al-Bistami: *Early Islamic Mysticism: Sufi, Qur'an, Mi'raj, Po-
etic and Theological Writings,* translated, edited, and with an introduction by Michael A. Sells, Paulist Press, 1996.

Bankei: *The Unborn: The Life and Teachings of Zen Master Bankei,
1622–1693,* translated and with an introduction by Norman Waddell,
North Point Press, 1984.

The Bible: *Genesis: A New Translation of the Classic Biblical Stories,*
Stephen Mitchell, HarperCollins, 1996; *The Book of Job,* translated
with an introduction by Stephen Mitchell, HarperCollins 1992; and
The Song of Songs, a new translation with an introduction and commentary by Ariel Bloch and Chana Bloch, Random House, 1995.

Blake: *The Portable Blake,* edited by Alfred Kazin, Penguin, 1946, and
The Complete Poetry and Prose of William Blake, edited by David V.

Erdman, commentary by Harold Bloom, University of California Press, 1982.

The Buddha: *Buddhism in Translations,* edited by Henry Clarke Warren, Dover, 1986; *What the Buddha Taught,* Walpola Rahula, Grove Press, 1959; *Buddhist Scriptures,* selected and translated by Edward Conze, Penguin, 1959; and *Teachings of the Buddha,* edited by Jack Kornfield with Gil Fronsdal, Shambhala, 1996.

Bunan: *The Original Face: An Anthology of Rinzai Zen,* translated and edited by Thomas Cleary, Grove Press, 1978, and *The Roaring Stream: A New Zen Reader,* edited by Nelson Foster and Jack Shoemaker, The Ecco Press, 1996 (under the entry Shidō Munan).

Catherine of Siena (1347–1380): *I, Catherine: Selected Writings of St. Catherine of Siena,* edited and translated by Kenelm Foster, O. P., and Mary John Ronayne, O. P., Collins, 1980.

Chuang-tzu: *The Way of Chuang Tzu,* Thomas Merton, New Directions, 1965; *The Complete Works of Chuang Tzu,* translated by Burton Watson, Columbia University Press, 1968; *The Book of Chuang Tzu,* translated by Martin Palmer, with Elizabeth Breuilly, Chang Wai Ming, and Jay Ramsay, Arkana, 1996; and *Chuang Tzu: The Inner Chapters,* translated by David Hinton, Counterpoint, 1997.

The Cloud of Unknowing: *The Cloud of Unknowing,* translated with an introduction by Clifton Wolters, Penguin, 1961, and *The Cloud of Unknowing,* edited and with an introduction by James Walsh, S. J., Paulist Press, 1981.

Confucius: *The Wisdom of Confucius,* translated by Lin Yutang, The Modern Library, 1938; *The Great Digest, the Unwobbling Pivot, and the Analects,* translation and commentary by Ezra Pound, New Directions, 1969; and *The Essential Confucius: The Heart of Confucius's Teachings in Authentic I Ching Order: A Compendium of Ethical Wisdom,* translated and presented by Thomas Cleary, HarperSanFrancisco, 1992.

The Diamond Sutra: *The Diamond Sutra and the Sutra of Hui Neng,* translated by A. F. Price and Wong Mou-Lam, Shambhala, 1969, and *The Diamond That Cuts Through Illusion: Commentaries on the Prajñaparamita Diamond Sutra,* Thich Nhat Hanh, Parallax Press, 1992.

Dōgen: *Moon in a Dewdrop,* edited by Kazuaki Tanahashi, North Point Press 1985; *How to Raise an Ox,* translated by Francis H. Cook, Center Publications, 1978; and *Sounds of Valley Streams,* translated by Francis H. Cook, State University of New York Press, 1989.

Meister Eckhart: *Breakthrough: Meister Eckhart's Creation Spirituality in New Translation,* introduction and commentaries by Matthew Fox, O. P., translations by Robert Cunningham, Ron Miller, Matthew Fox, Elizabeth Heptner, and Thomas O'Meara, Doubleday, 1980, and *Meister Eckhart, German Sermons and Treatises,* translated with introduction and notes by M. O'C. Walshe, vol. 1, Watkins, 1979; vol. 2, Watkins, 1981.

Einstein: *Out of My Later Years,* Philosophical Library, 1950.

Emerson: *The Complete Essays and Other Writings of Ralph Waldo Emerson,* edited by Brooks Atkinson, The Modern Library, 1940; *Selections from Ralph Waldo Emerson,* edited by Stephen E. Whicher, Houghton Mifflin, 1957; and *The Portable Emerson,* edited by Carl Bode in collaboration with Malcolm Cowley, Penguin, 1981.

The Gospel of Thomas: *The Nag Hammadi Library in English,* edited by James M. Robinson, Harper & Row, 1977, and *The Gospel of Thomas: The Hidden Sayings of Jesus,* translation, with introduction, critical edition of the Coptic text, and notes by Marvin Meyer, with an interpretation by Harold Bloom, HarperSanFrancisco, 1992.

Heraclitus: *The Art and Thought of Heraclitus: An Edition of the Fragments with Translation and Commentary,* Charles H. Kahn, Cambridge University Press, 1979, and *7 Greeks,* translations by Guy Davenport, New Directions, 1995.

Huang-po: *The Zen Teaching of Huang Po,* translated by John Blofeld, Grove Press, 1958, and *Original Teachings of Ch'an Buddhism,* Chang Chung-yuan, Pantheon, 1969.

Hui-hai: *The Zen Teaching of Hui Hai,* translated by John Blofeld, Rider & Company, 1962.

Jesus of Nazareth: *The Gospel According to Jesus: A New Translation and Guide to His Essential Teachings for Believers and Unbelievers,* Stephen Mitchell, HarperCollins, 1991, and *Meeting Jesus Again for the First Time: The Historical Jesus and the Heart of Contemporary Faith,* Marcus J. Borg, HarperSanFrancisco, 1994.

Julian of Norwich: *Revelations of Divine Love,* translated with an introduction by Clifton Wolters, Penguin, 1966, and *Showings,* translated with an introduction by Edmond Colledge, O. S. A., and James Walsh, S. J., Paulist Press, 1978.

Kafka: *Dearest Father: Stories and Other Writings,* translated by Ernst Kaiser and Eithne Wilkins, Schocken Books, 1954.

Kook: *Abraham Isaac Kook: The Lights of Penitence, the Moral Principles, Lights of Holiness, Essays, Letters, and Poems,* translation and introduction by Ben Zion Bokser, Paulist Press, 1978.

Lao-tzu: *Tao Te Ching, A New English Version,* Stephen Mitchell, Harper & Row, 1988.

Lin-chi: *The Zen Teachings of Master Lin-chi,* translated by Burton Watson, Shambhala, 1993, and *Original Teachings of Ch'an Buddhism,* Chang Chung-yuan, Pantheon, 1969.

Ma-tsu: *Sun Face Buddha: The Teachings of Ma-tsu and the Hung-chou School of Ch'an,* Cheng Chien Bhikshu, Asian Humanities Press, 1992, and *Original Teachings of Ch'an Buddhism,* Chang Chung-yuan, Pantheon, 1969.

Muhammad: *The Koran,* translated by N. J. Dawood, Penguin, 1968, and *The Essential Koran: An Introductory Selection of Readings from the Quran,* translated and presented by Thomas Cleary, HarperSanFrancisco, 1993.

Novalis: *Philosophical Writings,* translated and edited by Margaret Mahony Stoljar, State University of New York Press, 1997.

Padmasambhava: *The Tibetan Book of the Dead,* a new translation with commentary by Francesca Fremantle and Chögyam Trungpa, Shambhala, 1975, and *The Tibetan Book of the Great Liberation,* translated by W. Y. Evans-Wentz, Oxford University Press, 1954.

The Perfection of Wisdom Sutra: *Buddhist Texts through the Ages,* edited by Edward Conze, Shambhala, 1990.

Philo: *The Essential Philo,* edited by Nahum N. Glazer, Schocken, 1971, and *Philo of Alexandria: The Contemplative Life, the Giants, and Selections,* translation and introduction by David Winston, Paulist Press, 1981.

Ramana Maharshi: *Ramana Maharshi and the Path of Self-Knowledge,* Arthur Osborne, Weiser, 1973; *Be As You Are: The Teachings of Sri Ramana Maharshi,* edited by David Godman, Arkana, 1985; and *Talks with Sri Ramana Maharshi,* Munagala S. Venkataramiah (sixth edition), Sri Ramanasramam, 1978.

Rilke: *Ahead of All Parting: The Selected Poetry and Prose of Rainer Maria Rilke,* edited and translated by Stephen Mitchell, Modern Library, 1995, and *Letters to a Young Poet,* translated and with a foreword by Stephen Mitchell, Random House, 1984.

Ryōkan: *Ryōkan, Zen Poet-Monk of Japan,* translated by Burton Watson, Columbia University Press 1977, and *One Robe, One Bowl: The Zen Poetry of Ryōkan,* translated by John Stevens, Weatherhill, 1977.

Seng-ts'an: *Entering the Stream,* compiled and edited by Samuel Bercholz and Sherab Chödzin Kohn, Shambhala, 1993, and *The Roaring Stream: A New Zen Reader,* edited by Nelson Foster and Jack Shoemaker, The Ecco Press, 1996. The version in *The Enlightened Heart* includes about half of the original poem.

Spinoza: *The Collected Works of Spinoza, vol. 1,* edited and translated by Edwin Curley, Princeton University Press, 1985, and *Works of Spinoza,* translated by R. H. M. Elwes, Dover Publications, vol. 1, 1951; vol. 2, 1955.

Suzuki: *Zen Mind, Beginner's Mind,* Weatherhill, 1970.

Tung-shan: *The Record of Tung-shan,* translated by William F. Powell, University of Hawaii Press, 1986, and *Original Teachings of Ch'an Buddhism,* Chang Chung-yuan, Pantheon, 1969.

Tzu-ssu: *The Wisdom of Confucius,* translated by Lin Yutang, The Modern Library, 1938.

The Upanishads: *The Ten Principal Upanishads,* put into English by W. B. Yeats and Shree Purohit Swami, Macmillan 1937, and *The Upanishads,* translated by Eknath Easwaran, Nilgiri Press, 1987.

Wang Wei: *Laughing Lost in the Mountains: Poems of Wang Wei,* translations by Tony Barnstone, Willis Barnstone, and Xu Haixin, University Press of New England, 1991.

Weil: *Waiting for God,* translated by Emma Craufurd, Putnam, 1951; *Gravity and Grace,* translated by Emma Craufurd, Putnam, 1952; *Gate-*

way to God, edited by David Raper, Collins, 1974; *The Simone Weil Reader,* edited by George A. Panichas, McKay, 1977; and *Simone Weil: An Anthology,* edited and introduced by Siân Miles, Weidenfeld & Nicolson, 1986.

Wittgenstein: *Philosophical Investigations,* translated by G. E. M. Anscombe, Macmillan, 1968, and *The Blue and Brown Books,* Harper & Brothers, 1958.

Wu-men: *The Gateless Barrier,* Robert Aitken, North Point Press, 1991; *Gateless Gate,* Koun Yamada, Center Publications, 1979; and *Zen Comments on the Mumonkan,* Zenkei Shibayama, Harper & Row, 1974.

Yün-men: *Master Yunmen,* translated, edited, and with an introduction by Urs App, Kodansha International, 1994, and *Original Teachings of Ch'an Buddhism,* Chang Chung-yuan, Pantheon, 1969.

DATE DUE

PRINTED IN U.S.A.